Sid H

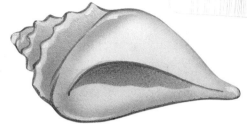

by Tim Buckwalter   **illustrated by Reggie Holladay**

Orlando   Boston   Dallas   Chicago   San Diego

Visit *The Learning Site!*

www.harcourtschool.com

Printed in China

ISBN 0-15-325438-6

8 9 10 121 10 09 08 07 06 05 04

Ordering Options
ISBN 0-15-323766-X (Collection)
ISBN 0-15-329610-0 (package of 5)

 Sid hid.
I can not see him.

 Did you look in the big box?

 I did. Sid is not in it.

3

Did you look in the red bag?
I did. Sid is not in it.

4

 Did you look in the tin can?
 I did. Sid is not in it.

Did you look in the big pot?
I did. Sid is not in it.

Did you look in his little shell?
I did not.

 Sid is in it.
Sid is in his shell!